Oleg Olegovich Yadrevsky

Geographical indications

Oleg Olegovich Yadrevsky

Geographical indications

Legal protection as intellectual property objects

ScienciaScripts

Imprint
Any brand names and product names mentioned in this book are subject to trademark, brand or patent protection and are trademarks or registered trademarks of their respective holders. The use of brand names, product names, common names, trade names, product descriptions etc. even without a particular marking in this work is in no way to be construed to mean that such names may be regarded as unrestricted in respect of trademark and brand protection legislation and could thus be used by anyone.

Cover image: www.ingimage.com

This book is a translation from the original published under ISBN 978-3-659-78476-7.

Publisher:
Sciencia Scripts
is a trademark of
Dodo Books Indian Ocean Ltd. and OmniScriptum S.R.L publishing group

120 High Road, East Finchley, London, N2 9ED, United Kingdom
Str. Armeneasca 28/1, office 1, Chisinau MD-2012, Republic of Moldova, Europe
Printed at: see last page
ISBN: 978-620-7-97302-6

TABLE OF CONTENTS:

INTRODUCTION

The concept of "geographical indication" can be considered, firstly, as any indication that either contains the name of a geographical object or otherwise creates an association with a geographical object; secondly, as a designation indicating the geographical place of origin of goods. In both cases legal protection of such designations may be exercised by means of intellectual property objects. At the same time, the legal regulation of this issue is extremely diverse in different legal systems, as well as in states and interstate formations. Legal protection of such designations has become increasingly important in recent years, which is reflected in scientific works and publications of researchers.

If we talk about the studies conducted by Western experts in this field, the main attention is paid to the World Trade Organisation Agreement on Trade-Related Aspects of Intellectual Property Rights of 1994 (hereinafter - TRIPS Agreement), which established the concept of "geographical indication" as an intellectual property object, reflecting the essential link between the properties of goods and their place of origin, the prerequisites for its adoption, scope of activity, correlation with other international treaties, acts of the European Union are considered Separate researchers consider in detail the history of the development of legal protection of geographical indications, noting their special significance as the first means of individualisation of goods, historically the first types of trademarks [1, p. 11]. It is argued that the modern system of protection of geographical indications was formed primarily due to the principles of liberalism and free competition, which began to be enshrined in the legislation since the late 19th century. [2, c. 125].

The role in the development of legal regulation of the object under consideration is defined such major agreements as the Paris Convention for the Protection of Industrial Property of 1883 (hereinafter - the Paris Convention) - in terms of protection against the use of false indications of origin, the Madrid Agreement for the Suppression of False or Misleading Indications of Origin on Goods of 1891 (hereinafter - the Madrid Agreement) - in terms of protection against the use of misleading indications of origin, the Lisbon Agreement for the Protection of Appellations of Origin and the Lisbon Agreement for the Protection of Appellations of Origin, and the Lisbon Agreement for the Protection of Appellations of Origin.

The studies under consideration identify the main ways to protect geographical indications: the rules on the prohibition of unfair competition, consumer protection rules, legislation on trademarks, collective and certification marks, special legislation on geographical indications [3, p. 5-6].

At the same time, it is pointed out that there are two approaches to the optimal protection of geographical indications: in the framework of sui generis legislation or in the framework of trademark law [4, p. 18].

At the same time, there are concerns that the system of protection of trademarks and geographical indications formed in the 1990s may lead to disregard for the protection of free competition and the possibility of granting appropriate protection to new entities [5, p. 23]. Thus, one of the most problematic issues in this area is the relationship between a trademark, which is or contains a geographical indication, and a geographical indication. At the same time, the principle "first in time - first in law" is considered to be the most appropriate in this matter, because it is able to create "a fair mechanism of balance between conflicting intellectual property rights" [3, p. 38]. [3, c. 38].

With regard to the studies carried out in the territory of the former USSR, the following should be noted. In Soviet times, little attention was paid to the legal protection of geographical indications, including geographical indications. This was primarily due to the lack of legislative regulation of these issues. Some publications concerning the legal protection of geographical indications (e.g., the work of G.I. Tytskaya, I.E. Mamiofa, V.Y. Motylov, 1985) are devoted to the consideration of the legislation of capitalist states and international treaties, without applying the relevant results to the norms of the law of the USSR [6].

Since the 1990s, the Russian Federation has been conducting more in-depth studies of these issues. Thus, numerous works by A.N. Grigoriev are devoted to the issues of legal protection of geographical indications. The author substantiates the necessity of legal regulation of the use of indications of origin of goods by the norms of civil law, specifies the criteria of protectability of indications of origin of goods, argues the need for their registration. The author suggests the idea that the term "indications of origin" applies only to goods with special properties due to the place of origin. It is pointed out that it is necessary to create a state system of control over the quality of goods designated by the protected appellation of origin. When registering the appellation of origin of goods, according to ANTrigoriev, it is necessary to provide evidence that the goods are fully produced and processed in the specified place. A methodology for assessing the possibility of registration as a trademark of a geographical designation is proposed [7, p. 10-11].

The central place in the works of Satorlenko in the period under review is given to such an object as the appellation of origin of goods. The history of the development of protection of this object, its current state in the Russian Federation, as well as existing problematic aspects are considered in detail. Particular attention is paid to the need to create an effective system of control over the properties of goods, as well as to improve the mechanism for obtaining a conclusion of the competent authority on the applicant's production of goods with special properties due exclusively or mainly to the place of origin [8].

In the 2000s, the number of studies on the issues under consideration increased. Thus, E.A. Danilina and EL. Gavrilov attempted to identify the most significant problems in the legal protection of the appellation of origin of goods. The authors note that "in the list of intellectual property objects distributed by their economic (national economic) importance, where the enumeration begins with the most important, appellations of origin of goods until recently firmly occupied a not very honourable last place, sharing it with topologies of integrated circuits. This illustrates the extent to which the [Russian] economy lags behind the developed countries of the world: the most culturally significant and, in fact, practically priceless object (appellation of origin) and the most high-tech object (integrated circuit topology) turned out to be outsiders of industrial property rights registration" [9]. [9].

Among the most significant problems of the legal protection of the appellation of origin of goods the authors name: the question of the possibility of extending the legal protection of appellations of origin of goods to the sphere of services, active parallel obtaining of various protection documents along with certificates for the right to use the appellation of origin of goods: both certificates for trademarks, including names, and patents for inventions and industrial designs; the need for the identity of special properties of goods, individualised in the name of the place of origin of goods; the necessity of the right to use the appellation of origin of goods; the necessity of the right to use the appellation of origin of goods in the sphere of services. The issues of the content of the exclusive right to the appellation of origin of goods are also studied. Public-law elements of the appellation of origin of goods, in particular, the need to obtain the opinion of the competent authority, are singled out. At the same time, despite the identification of problematic aspects, the authors in many cases do not offer specific ways to solve them, inviting interested parties to the discussion.

The issues of legal protection of the appellation of origin of goods are also studied by V.E.Kitaysky, who substantiates the inexpediency of termination of the registration of the appellation of origin of goods in case of termination of all certificates for the right to use the appellation of origin of goods. In addition, the author strongly opposes the above-mentioned practice of resolving disputes between a trademark consisting or containing a geographical indication and the appellation of origin of goods, based on the principle of "first in time - first in law" [10, p. 23]. [10, c. 23].

In the Russian Federation a number of PhD theses devoted to the legal protection of means of individualisation of goods containing geographical indications (M.N. Sokolova), appellations of origin of goods (M.A. Saltykov) have been prepared [11, 12]. In addition, a number of dissertations on the legal protection of national geographical indications are defended (G.A. Takhirov (Tajikistan), M.A. Kharkhipova (Ukraine), N.V. Chang (Vietnam)) [13,14,15]. [13,14,15].

Distinctive features of most of these works are attempts to clearly define the concepts of "geographical indication", "indication of origin of goods", "appellation of origin of goods", proposals on the need to use the experience of legal regulation of these objects in the EU countries.

It should be noted that recently at the level of Rospatent there have been expressed views on the need to include geographical indication in the meaning of the TRIPS Agreement in the composition of protected industrial property objects with its registration [16, p. 17].

As for the issues of legal protection of trademarks representing or containing designations of the geographical place of origin of goods, they are also considered in numerous articles by Russian scientists and practitioners.

Thus, in the mentioned dissertation research of M.N. Sokol, an attempt was made to form a classification of designations of geographical place of origin of goods, which can be granted legal protection as trademarks, in order to use it in practice. In the dissertations of N.Y. Medvedev and P.V. Sadovsky the practice of Rospatent on this issue is analysed, the need to improve the legal regulation of these relations is acknowledged [17, 18]. Quite detailed issues of connection and distinction of a trademark from the designations of geographical place of origin of goods are considered in the works of A.P. Rabets, V.M. Melnikov [19, 20]. At the same time, these works contain few practical proposals for a clearer regulation of these aspects.

The concept of "distinctive ability" in relation to this issue is analysed in the works of M.N. Zubkova and V.Y. Jermakyan [21, 22]. The interest of practitioners to this problem is characteristic, in particular, here we can note the articles by ML.Epstein and I.V. Rogal [23,24].

At the same time, some issues have not been covered in Russian-language studies either. In particular, it concerns the possibility of registration of a collective mark representing a designation of geographical place of origin, which is common in the EU. Also insufficient attention is paid to the issues of correlation between a trade mark representing or containing the designation of geographical place of origin of goods and the appellation of origin of goods, which, as noted above, is a serious subject of research among Western specialists.

In connection with the above, it seems necessary to analyse these works on some issues in the field of legal protection of geographical indications as intellectual property objects. This paper will initially consider the historical development of such protection. Later on, more detailed attention will be paid to the individual objects by means of which this protection is realised. The positions of some German, Russian and other experts in this field will be analysed.

CHAPTER 1

HISTORICAL DEVELOPMENT OF THE LEGAL PROTECTION OF GEOGRAPHICAL INDICATIONS

Even in the pre-industrial era, small-scale production of products (above all wine and cheese) emerged and developed, and it was customary to specify the locality from which they originated in order to better characterise their properties.

For example, in the 4th century B.C. the designations of wines from Greece include Corinthian, Corsican, Rhodesian wines. In addition, since ancient times Sicilian honey, Desemian vinegar are known; by the reign of Augustus in the Roman Empire, Falernian wine, Egyptian dates, Gallic ham, etc. became famous. [8, c. 4 - 5].

At the beginning of the 8th century AD, the oldest wine-growing regions of France appeared: Bordeaux, Burgundy, and later Champagne. The Middle Ages also saw the emergence of the cheese-making regions of Camembert and Roquefort (France), Emmentaler (Switzerland), Parma (Parmesan) (Italy). Apart from agricultural products, other types of goods originating from a particular locality became famous: Havana tobacco, Darjeeling tea, Sheffield steel, etc. Due to their features and quality, Scottish whisky, Cuban rum, Bavarian beer, Ceylon tea, Brazilian coffee, Parisian perfume, carpets of India, Persia, etc. become recognisable. [25, c. 24].

The advantage of using the designation of geographical place of origin over other designations was explained by the fact that products from specific regions had special properties that similar products from other places did not have. These properties were attributed to the climate, the soils, as well as to the secrets of production and the special knowledge and skills of the people in the area, which had been passed down from generation to generation. Over time, some of these products became known and popular far beyond the borders of their countries and regions.

Thus, geographical indications, which can be defined as designations of the geographical place of origin of a product with properties determined to a significant extent by its geographical origin, can be called the very first means of individualisation, because their widespread use began earlier than the use of a brand name or trademark [26, p. 388].

Apparently, the widespread use of geographical indications for individualisation of goods of specific manufacturers in the absence of mass production has led to a widespread view in foreign literature that geographical indications can be considered as the earliest form of trademarks [32, p. 303]. In this case, apparently, trademarks here should be understood in the broad sense of the word, as a distinctive designation of a particular product, and not in the modern legal meaning of the term.

Already in the Middle Ages in Europe, the first legal acts concerning geographical indications began to be developed. An example here is the Charter of the Yugoslav King Stefan I, issued in 1222, which regulated the sale of wine [3, p. 3]. In 1411 the French king Charles VI honoured the inhabitants of Roquefort with the monopoly right to make cheese in local caves. This decree forbade to call Roquefort other similar cheeses [4, p. 166]. Some producers of goods obtain a monopoly right to use a geographical indication on their products by obtaining privileges from the supreme power. Such designations are often used as the so-called "guild mark", which individualises the goods of an association of producers. Many of these signs are still widespread today, for example, the designation of glass "Migalo", originating from the island of the same name near Venice (Italy) [3, p. 3].

In addition to "direct" geographical indications, i.e. those that directly indicate the geographical place of production of a product, so-called "indirect" geographical indications are beginning to appear, which also receive legal protection. Thus, in the 15th century, bladed knives from Solingen (Germany) began to be labelled with the image of a wolf. This image later became known as the Solingen wolf. And although it did not directly contain the designation of the geographical place of origin of goods, however, only the manufacturers of bladed knives from Solingen could use such a mark, while manufacturers from other regions were not entitled to mark this designation [2, p. 16].

At the same time, the issuance of privileges served the main purpose of asserting the monopoly of this or that workshop or craftsman. At the same time, there were no effective means of combating unfair competition, which was already beginning to spread at this time in the area of geographical indications in the labelling of goods. Laws containing provisions prohibiting false indications in the labelling of goods began to appear in Western Europe only in the 19th century. However, they did not deal specifically with geographical indications, but only with false labelling in general. As an example, we can cite the Prussian Law on the Protection of Goods Designations of 4 July 1840, which contained a ban on the use of a false name or company name together with the indication of the place of residence of this person or the location of the factory [2, p. 18].

Thus, at the first stage, legal protection of geographical indications was only fragmented in some countries. In the first stage, legal protection of geographical indications was only fragmentary in some countries.

The development of industrial production in Europe, the increase in the number of subjects of the production process, often within the same geographical area, as well as their increasing specialisation, lead to the desire to individualise the goods of a particular manufacturer. As a consequence of this, such means of individualisation as a trademark was legislated. In 1857 France adopted a law on trade marks. Until 1900, 7 more countries adopted national regulations on the legal protection of trademarks [28]. In order to obtain legal protection of trademarks abroad, the Madrid Agreement on the International Registration of Marks was concluded on 14 April 1891 [29].

Thus, there is a gradual evolution of means of individualisation from more general, such as geographical indications, to more specific. As rightly noted in the monograph of the German researcher O. Spuhler, trademarks become a means of individualisation not of the manufacturer of goods and not of the place of origin, but of the production origin of goods [5, p. 43]. It includes along with the manufacturer and place of production of goods also many additional factors, such as production technology, quality control system, etc. The main criterion for the protectability of a trademark becomes distinctiveness and lack of need for free use. Since a geographical indication, having a certain distinctiveness (limited by the territory of the geographical object), still cannot be "monopolised" by a single manufacturer or even a group of manufacturers, the said laws on trademarks begin to enshrine restrictions, according to which the designation of the place of origin of goods cannot be registered as a trademark.

In 1883, the very first and to date the largest international agreement in the field of industrial property protection, the Paris Convention for the Protection of Industrial Property (hereinafter referred to as the Paris Convention), was signed. Article 10 of the Paris Convention in its original version provided for seizure of a product upon importation, prohibition of importation or seizure on the territory of the country in case of use on it of a false indication of origin (direct or indirect), but only if such indication was used with a trade mark of a counterfeit nature or with the purpose of deception [30].

At the Rome Conference in 1886, delegates attempted to strengthen the provisions of Article 10 of the Paris Convention by prohibiting the use of any false indications of origin and by giving the national courts of the countries of the Union the right to determine which of the indications of origin had become generic or descriptive in their territory. However, these proposals, although adopted, were not ratified by the Member States of the Union. These issues were raised again at the Madrid Conference of 1890. The result was the Madrid Agreement for the Suppression of False Indications of Origin on Goods (hereinafter referred to as the Madrid Agreement) [31], which was concluded in 1891. This agreement was, in turn, the first international document that defined indications of origin as its subject matter. The Agreement extended their legal protection, since in order to recognise an indication of origin as false, it was no longer necessary to use it together with a trademark or intent to defraud. The provisions of the Agreement applied to any goods that travelled between two Contracting Parties to the Agreement, regardless of where the abusive indication was added and regardless of the nationality of the defendant.

At the Washington Diplomatic Conference in 1911, an indication of origin was included in Article 1(2) of the Paris Convention as an independent object of industrial property. However, unlike other industrial property objects, such as trademarks or inventions, the Paris Convention did not stipulate that indications of origin had to be registered in order to be granted legal protection, that they had to have an owner or a specifically defined circle of owners, etc. Their protection was intended only to prevent the use of false indications of origin, i.e., it was aimed more at protecting the rights of consumers and much less at protecting the rights of specific producers.

It should be noted that in 1958, the Madrid Agreement was amended to prohibit the use of indications of origin that are formally true but can be misleading (for example, the names of small American cities similar to the names of European capitals - Paris, London, etc.).

However, it should be noted that only 36 States are currently participating in the Madrid Agreement, the reasons for which will be discussed further below.

Thus, by the beginning of the 20th century, the first object of industrial property, by means of which geographical indications were protected, - the indication of origin - had been formalised at the international level. Consequently, we can speak of the beginning of the second stage in the legal protection of geographical indications.

At the same time, the existing limited legal protection of the designation of origin did not suit some European countries with rich traditions of winemaking and agricultural production (France, Italy, Spain, Portugal), because the use of a well-known designation of origin of such products even without the purpose of deception or misleading, but, for example, with the addition of the words "type", "genus", "kind", "species" could lead to the "blurring" of the designation and turn it into a generic concept, which prevented the possibility of its legal protection At the same time, it was also difficult to register such a designation as a trademark due to the above-mentioned restrictions [8, p. 6]. In addition, the goods could originate from the specified area, but not have special properties due to the place of their origin.

All this led to the birth of a new object of industrial property, which is most often referred to as the appellation of origin. The first law on the protection of the appellation of origin was adopted on 6 May 1919 in France. For a long time it was applied only to wines and spirits, but later it was extended to other goods (dairy products, poultry, products of plant origin). According to this law, the appellation of origin was defined as the name of a country, district or locality which serves to designate a commodity originating in that country, district or locality and whose quality and characteristics are determined exclusively or mainly by the geographical environment, including natural conditions and human factors.

Following the example of France, the same or similar system was also introduced in other countries, mainly in relation to wines and spirits (Italian Law of 10 April 1954 No. 125 "On the use of typical names of cheeses", Italian Law of 7 December 1951 No. 1618 on the protection of names of certain types of wines) [32,33].

In 1925, at the Hague Diplomatic Conference for the revision of the Paris Convention, appellations of origin were included as an object of industrial property.

Since that time, we can speak of the beginning of the third stage of the legal protection of geographical indications.

The main difference between the appellation of origin and the designation of origin was that the former could only be applied to goods with special properties due exclusively or mainly to the geographical environment, whereas there was no such requirement for designations of origin. This difference determined, firstly, the necessity to confirm such properties through registration of the appellation of origin, and secondly, the scope of legal protection. The main purpose of granting legal protection to this object was to protect producers of such unique, specific goods from "dilution" of the designation and its transformation into a generic concept.

With the development of the legal protection of the appellation of origin of goods at the international level, work began on the creation of a special international agreement, which would, on the one hand, serve as a basis for the creation in other states of national legislation in the field of protection of the appellation of origin of goods, on the other hand, would be aimed at harmonising national provisions on the protection of geographical indications in general and the appellation of origin of goods in particular. Such an agreement was signed in the city of Lisbon on 31 October 1958 and was called the Lisbon Agreement for the Protection of Appellations of Origin and their International Registration (hereinafter referred to as the Lisbon Agreement). In it, for the first time at the international level, a full and clear definition of the appellation of origin was given. This definition with some modifications was adopted by many national laws. At the same time, rather strict conditions for granting legal protection to the appellation of origin in accordance with the Lisbon Agreement were the reason why it did not gain much popularity in the world. To date, 28 states participate in the Lisbon Agreement [34].

The system of protection of geographical indications is further developed at the regional level within the European Economic Community (hereinafter - EEC), when the member states face the problem of using identical names traditionally protected in two or even more EEC countries. Until 1992, there was no unified approach to the protection of geographical indications within the EEC, except for the provisions on protection against false or misleading indications of origin and prohibition of unfair competition. On 14 July 1992, EEC Regulation No 2081/92 on the Protection of Geographical Indications and Appellations of Origin of Agricultural Products and Foodstuffs (hereinafter referred to as Regulation No 2081/92) was adopted and entered into force on 24 July 1993. This document established the first major regional system for the protection of geographical indications. The main innovation was the introduction of a new protected entity called protected geographical indication (PGI) alongside the already existing term protected designation of origin (PDO). Both terms are used only in relation to agricultural products and foodstuffs and are defined as the name of a geographical entity (a region, a particular locality, a country) that is used to designate an agricultural product or foodstuff with a special quality or characteristics that are due mainly or exclusively to geographical factors, including natural and human influences. At the same time, in order to grant legal protection to an appellation of origin, the said products must be produced, processed, or manufactured within that geographical entity, whereas for registration of a geographical indication it is sufficient that only one of the stages of the production process is carried out within that geographical entity. At the same time, the scope of legal protection of the two objects is the same [35].

This Regulation was replaced on 20 March 2006 by the EU Council Regulation on the Legal Protection of Geographical Indications and Designations of Origin of Agricultural and Foodstuffs No. 510/2006 (hereinafter - Regulation No. 510/2006), which also uses the above terminology. At the same time, this Regulation introduces another object - "guaranteed compliance with the traditional recipe", the definition of which differs from the above two terms by the absence of an indication of the geographical origin of the product [36]. Currently, the EU Regulation No. 1151/2012 of the European Parliament and of the Council of 21 November 2012 (hereinafter - Regulation No. 1151/2012) is in force on this issue [37].

However, even within the European Union, not all national laws currently provide for the protection of these types of geographical indications. Here we can speak of the existence of two systems of national legislation: the German system, according to which "simple" geographical indications (i.e., indications of origin) are protected, and the French system, which gives legal protection to "qualified" geographical indications (i.e., protected appellations of origin and geographical indications) and which is the basis for the above-mentioned Regulations [38, p. 122].

It should be noted, however, that the evolution of the legal protection of geographical indications discussed above refers to the countries of the Romano-Germanic legal family (France, Spain, Germany, Italy). At the same time, in the countries of the so-called "common law" (in particular, in the USA) there is no special legal regulation for such designations. In this area, only legislation against unfair competition (against so-called "passing off" acts) is in force, which is combined with the registration of geographical indications under trademark law. Due to the fact that, as mentioned above, trademark law often contains restrictions on the registration of a designation of geographical place of origin as a trademark, the certification mark system is widely used in these countries. A certification mark is a designation (verbal, pictorial, etc.), the right to use which is granted by a certain public authority only to those producers who fulfil certain requirements. Such requirements are reflected in the specification for the certification mark and may consist of the need to produce goods within a specific geographical area. Unlike trademarks, certification marks can be affixed by any manufacturer of a certain type of goods, if it is produced in the relevant area (for example, the certification mark "FJ" for fruit juices produced in Florida) [6, c. 69].

Thus, by the end of the twentieth century, several major systems for the protection of geographical indications had emerged in the world:

1.   "German". The main means of protecting geographical indications is the protection of indications of origin.

2.   "French". In addition to indications of origin, legal protection is granted to the appellation of origin of goods to designate goods with special properties.

Since the "German" system is more characteristic of the Nordic countries and the "French" system of Southern Europe, the EEC has attempted to unify these systems under Regulation No. 2081/92.

3.   "American" (this name was introduced due to the fact that the majority of goods from the countries of this system, on which geographical indications are applied, originate from the USA). Geographical indications are protected under the legislation on counteracting unfair competition and the legislation on trade marks. The certification mark system is widespread.

In view of this difference in the legal regulation of geographical indications, since 1974 WIPO has sought to conclude an international agreement in this field that would harmonise the different systems of legal protection. At the centre of the regulation of this agreement was to be the concept of a "geographical indication", which is considered to be any designation of the actual place of production of a good, regardless of whether the characteristics of the good are linked to its geographical origin. Unfortunately, no such agreement has been concluded to date.

However, in 1994, a new important development in the protection of geographical indications took place. The emerging World Trade Organisation concluded one of its basic agreements, the Agreement on Trade-Related Aspects of Intellectual Property Rights (TRIPS), which defined minimum standards for the protection of the main intellectual property objects. A separate chapter of TRIPS is devoted to the regulation of a new object - geographical indication, which is defined in Article 22 as a designation reflecting a significant degree of association of the quality, reputation or other characteristics of a product with its geographical origin. With respect to such designations, TRIPS provides provisions on the prohibition of misleading consumers as to the true place of origin. It is specifically noted that such a designation may reflect the true place of origin but give a false impression to the public that the product originates from a different place [39].

In September 2008, the Assembly of the Lisbon Union established the Working Group on the Development of the Lisbon System, responsible for studying possible ways to improve the procedures within the Lisbon System to make it more attractive to users and potential new members, while maintaining the principles and objectives of the Lisbon Agreement [40].

The Diplomatic Conference for the adoption of the revised Lisbon Agreement took place from 11 to 21 May 2015. And on 20 May 2015, at the WIPO Diplomatic Conference, the Geneva Act on Appellations of Origin and Geographical Indications (hereinafter referred to as the Geneva Act), which constitutes the amended Lisbon Agreement, was signed by WIPO and States [41].

According to Article 2 of the Geneva Act, an appellation of origin means an appellation protected in a Contracting Party of origin which is the name of a geographical area, or other appellation known to indicate such an area, or containing such a name or other appellation, which serves to designate a product as originating in that geographical area, where the quality or characteristics of the product are due exclusively or mainly to the geographical environment, including natural and human factors.

As we can see, in comparison with the current version of the Lisbon Agreement, the definition of the appellation of origin of goods is broader, as it allows granting legal protection not only to a direct, but also to an indirect designation.

At the same time, Article 2 of the Geneva Act defines a geographical indication as an indication protected in the Contracting Party of origin which is the name of a geographical area or other indication known to indicate such an area, or which contains such a name or other indication which identifies the goods as originating in that geographical area, where a certain quality, reputation or other characteristic of the goods is due principally to their geographical origin [41].

Thus, in the evolution of the legal protection of geographical indications, four main stages can be clearly distinguished: at the first stage (from the 14th century to the beginning of the 20th century), the legal protection of certain geographical indications begins to be enshrined in the legislation of some states with the main purpose of asserting the monopoly of the manufacturer of products, while their legal protection as objects of intellectual property law is absent; at the second stage (the beginning of the 20th century - the middle of the 20th century) in the framework of the concept of "indication of origin of goods" as an object of intellectual property law. This evolution reflects the process of understanding, first at the national and then at the international level, of the essence and necessity of protection of geographical indications.

CHAPTER 2

THE CONDITIONS FOR GRANTING GEOGRAPHICAL INDICATIONS LEGAL PROTECTION AS INTELLECTUAL PROPERTY OBJECTS

Indication of origin

As noted above, legal protection of this object is provided by the Paris Convention. At present, the number of parties to the Paris Convention is 176 States, hence it is the most widespread means of legal protection of geographical indications.

At the same time, neither the Paris Convention itself nor the authoritative commentary to it by G. Bodenhausen specifies whether its provisions apply to all indications of the place of actual origin [42].

There are two main points of view on this issue. According to the first of them, an indication of origin is nothing more than information about the actual place of production of the goods, regardless of whether any of their properties are related to geographical origin [5, p. 3,14, p. 14]. The same approach dominates in authoritative WIPO publications [43, p. 237], besides, it is adhered to by the famous Russian civilist A.P. Sergeev [44, p. 385]. Meanwhile, it is noted that according to the traditionally used terminology the term "indication of origin" includes all appellations of origin of goods, but in its general use it has become rather a designation applied to those indications of origin that are not considered to be appellations of origin of goods [43, p. 237].

The second point of view is that the indication of origin applies only to goods whose properties are to some extent conditioned by the place of origin, which is known to consumers. In particular, this point of view is held by A Grigoriev. He justifies it by the fact that the first and fundamental prerequisite for the protection of geographical indications is the necessity to protect the designation, generally perceived as an indication of the geographical origin of the goods, which, if used in relation to goods originating from another place, will mislead the consumer as to the place of origin. In his view, "in reality, we can speak of an indication of origin as a legal category only when there is an established reputation of that product in relation to a given geographical place. As practice shows, the mere fact that an enterprise has chosen a particular geographical place for its activities (production or provision of services) does not make this geographical name an indication of origin of goods" [45, p. 17]. [45, c. 17].

This provision applies in particular to the practice of protection of designations of origin in Germany, where the average consumer's perception of a designation as geographical is decisive for it to be recognised as such. If the designation is not well known and is not perceived by the consumer as geographical, the provisions on protection against false geographical indications do not apply [46].

One can agree with this point of view in the sense that the prohibition of false or misleading indications of origin of goods, based on the essence of this concept, is primarily aimed at protecting the interests of consumers. However, if consumers do not associate with such an indication any properties, even if of a general nature (for example, high quality of any German goods), then there is no need to talk about violation of their rights.

At the same time, A. Grigoriev further makes the following conclusion. "A geographical appellation can become an indication of origin or even an appellation of origin only in the course of an enterprise's activities and only when the consumer develops a clear relationship between the place of production or sale of goods and their properties. Otherwise, the geographical name is only able to highlight the goods, not the place of its origin" [47, p. 18] [47, c. 18].

This raises the following question: how to determine the point at which the consumer develops such a relationship? It is quite possible that a product is produced in the territory of a little-known geographical area and that its properties are to a certain extent determined by the place of origin (for example, a newly discovered mineral water spring). If such a name is not granted legal protection within the framework of the prohibition of false designations, it may lead to significant damage, first of all, to the genuine producers of such goods, because in the case of unauthorised use of such a designation, over time consumers will develop a false relationship to the place of production of the goods.

At the same time, with regard to misleading the consumer (Madrid Agreement), the geographical object must be known, since a formally true indication of the place of origin may give rise to misconceptions about its origin, leading to a further misconception about the properties of the goods.

Thus, we believe that the legal protection of designations of origin is primarily aimed at protecting goods whose properties are to a certain extent determined by their place of origin. It does not matter whether consumers have a relevant relationship between the origin of goods and their properties (subjective criterion), the main thing is that such a relationship should exist objectively (objective criterion). However, this conclusion applies only to the prohibition of false indications of origin. As for misleading indications, they apply only to goods where there is such a relationship in the minds of consumers. Thus, both objective and subjective criteria are present in this case. As noted above, the prohibition of misleading indications of origin is enshrined in the Madrid Agreement. However, compared to the Paris Convention, the number of parties to the Madrid Agreement is small. The reasons are mainly due to the fact that agreements of this kind have difficulties in establishing and defining a specific area that would be suitable for a geographical indication, as well as difficulties in determining when a designation has become so widespread that it has become generic and descriptive. At the same time, the Madrid Agreement involves major European states such as Germany, France, the United Kingdom, Italy, Sweden, Switzerland [31].

At the same time, international, regional and national legislation, as well as publications to date, replace the concept of "designation of origin" with the term "geographical indication" within the meaning of the TRIPS Agreement.

Geographical indication

The concept of "geographical indication", as defined in the TRIPS Agreement above, is used only for goods of a certain quality, reputation or other characteristics that have a significant link to geographical origin. At the same time, legal protection is granted to both direct and indirect designations. It can be inferred from the content of Article 22(2) of the TRIPS Agreement that such protection is granted both against all acts that constitute acts of unfair competition and against any use that is likely to mislead consumers as to the geographical origin of the product.

It follows that a geographical indication within the meaning of the TRIPS Agreement is an object of industrial property right, and for most goods the legal regime for the protection of geographical indications is similar to the corresponding legal regime for indications of origin under the Paris Convention and the Madrid Agreement. In both cases, only an objective criterion is mandatory, i.e., the geographical origin of the goods, and in the case of designations capable of misleading the subjective criterion is also mandatory. At the same time, it should be noted that the definition of a geographical indication in the TRIPS Agreement contains the notion of a "significant degree" of conditioning of the properties of goods by their geographical origin, which is absent for designations of origin. Thus, on the official website of WIPO in the section "Geographical Indications. Frequently Asked Questions" notes that, unlike geographical indications within the meaning of the TRIPS Agreement, an indication of origin "does not imply the existence of special qualities, reputation or characteristics of a product that are substantially due to its place of origin" [48]. [48]. At the same time, as we noted earlier, an objective criterion is also necessary for an indication of origin, but the characteristics of a product can be linked to its geographical origin only in a very general way.

In addition, the concept of "geographical origin" is interpreted by some authors only as the conditionality of the properties of goods by natural conditions [1].

Thus, in view of the above, we believe that the concept of "geographical indication" within the meaning of the TRIPS Agreement is somewhat narrower than the concept of "indication of origin" under the Paris Convention.

In addition, Article 23 of the TRIPS Agreement provides an additional scope of legal protection for geographical indications for wines and spirits. The scope of their legal protection is close to such an object as "appellation of origin of goods". Thus, in addition to the general prohibitions common to all geographical indications, so-called delocalising clauses ("type", "kind", "genus", etc.) are prohibited. However, the prohibition is used only in relation to goods not originating from the territory of the designated geographical entity and only in relation to homogeneous goods, i.e. wines and spirits respectively.

At the same time, the TRIPS Agreement does not provide for the mandatory registration of geographical indications. This distinguishes them from the similar term enshrined in Regulation 1151/2012, despite the similarity of definitions. In this regard, it is difficult to agree with N.V. Chang, who identifies these concepts [15, p. 17]. The same can be said about the concept of "geographical indication" in the sense of the Geneva Act, which requires registration for granting legal protection and which will be discussed in more detail below.

We believe that the introduction of the concept of "geographical indication" in the TRIPS Agreement is due to the need, despite the noted differences in the legal regime of such designations in different states, to introduce a certain minimum level of their legal protection.

Name of place of origin of goods

According to Article 2(1) of the current version of the Lisbon Agreement, an appellation of origin means the geographical name of a country, region or locality which serves to designate a product which originates in that country, region or locality and whose quality and characteristics are determined exclusively or mainly by the geographical environment, including natural and human factors [49].

It should be noted that this definition has been criticised in foreign literature, mainly due to the presence of the concept of "geographical environment" in it. In the definition of appellation of origin and the rationale for the Lisbon Agreement, it is not clear whether both natural and human factors must be proven simultaneously or whether proof of the social factor alone is sufficient to satisfy the requirements of the concept. The properties of manufactured or artisanal goods may not be due to the natural conditions of the place of origin. On this issue, O.V.Ionova refers to the opinion of some foreign observers (P.K.Beier), according to which there is a fear that foreign authorities and courts may refuse to protect the appellation of origin for certain goods on the grounds that there is no necessary connection between the properties of the goods and the natural conditions of the place of origin. In addition, an example is given of a French court decision that refused to protect the name "Moutarde de Dijon" (mustard from Dijon) on the grounds that the raw material for mustard production can be obtained not only in Dijon and there is no qualitative link between the properties of mustard and the natural conditions of Dijon [50, p. 14].

It is also suggested that a qualitative relationship between a commodity and the geographical environment "which may have existed at the beginning of the manufacture of an industrial product may later be
"stretched" to the point where its existence is difficult to prove". Also in the light of migration processes, "traditions in production and skilled labour can be shifted from one geographical area to another" [43, p. 246] [43, c. 246]. This provision is one of the main reasons for the low popularity of the Lisbon Agreement in the world and the need to adopt the Geneva Act.

There are, however, other points of view on this issue. Thus, the theory often distinguishes "natural" appellations of origin, when the properties of goods are conditioned by natural factors; appellations of origin, where the properties of goods are conditioned only by human factors (there is no special name, but it is noted that such appellations of origin can be unstable, temporary and under certain conditions turn into species designations); "classical" appellations of origin, when the properties of goods are conditioned by natural factors; "classical" appellations of origin, when the properties of goods are conditioned by human factors (there is no special name, but it is noted that such appellations of origin can be unstable, temporary and under certain conditions turn into species designations). [26, c. 402]. Consequently, we can talk about an expansive interpretation of this concept.

We believe that this point of view requires more careful consideration. Here it is necessary to refer to the EU norms. As already mentioned above, the current EU Regulation No. 1151/2012 distinguishes two types of protected geographical indications for agricultural products and foodstuffs: Protected Designation of Origin (PDO) and Protected Geographical Indication (PGI). The former requires that all stages of the production process be carried out in the territory of the designated geographical feature, while for the latter it is sufficient that at least one of the stages be carried out in that territory. The scope of legal protection is the same.

According to V. Stoppel, the conceptual confusion is due to the different philosophies of the EEC Member States. The appellation of origin is more in line with the approaches of the Southern European countries - Spain and Italy, which relate geographical data to a product if its quality is directly acquired in a particular area. For example, this is the case for fruit grown and harvested there, milk and dairy products whose properties depend on the nutritional characteristics of the animals in a particular region, and wine. In contrast, geographical indication is more in line with the Northern European approach, according to which quality is determined by the know-how and experience of the producer, even if the raw material originates from another locality [51, p. 139].

For example, examples of protected German PDOs include meat from Luneburger Heidschnucke (Luneburger Heidschnucke), Allgauer Emmentaler (Allgauer Emmentaler) [52]. At the same time, the range of protected PGIs is much wider and includes, in particular, Bavarian and Dortmund beer (Bayerisches Bier, Dortmunder Bier), Schwarzwalder Schinken (Schwarzwalder Schinken), Liibecker Marzipan (Liibecker Marzipan) [53].

Thus, the above view of the concept of appellation of origin combines the features of PDO and PGI. At the same time, it does not limit the possibility of registering an appellation of origin to the sphere of agricultural and food products.

This broader definition of the appellation of origin is characteristic, in particular, of the legislation of the Russian Federation. According to Article 1516 of the Russian Civil Code, "the appellation of origin of goods, which is granted legal protection, is a designation that represents or contains a modern or historical, official or unofficial, full or abbreviated name of a country, urban or rural settlement, locality or other geographical object, as well as a designation derived from such a name and became known as a result of its use in relation to goods, the special properties of which are excluded from legal protection". [54].

It may be noted that this definition, by analogy with the Geneva Act, expands the list of designations that may be registered as an appellation of origin of goods. Thus, in addition to a designation representing the name of a geographical object, legal protection may be granted to designations containing the name of a geographical object, derivatives of the name of a geographical object, as well as designations not containing the name of an object but allowing to identify the goods as originating from the territory of a certain geographical object.

It should be noted that this definition is set out in Section VII of Annex 26 - Protocol on the Protection and Enforcement of Intellectual Property Rights - to the Treaty on the Eurasian Economic Union (EAEU), which entered into force on 1 January 2015. [55]. The EAEU currently comprises Armenia, Belarus, Kazakhstan, Kyrgyzstan and Russia.

At the same time, the peculiarity of the appellation of origin of goods is the necessity for such designation to be known, which is also stipulated by the Lisbon Agreement, according to Article 2 (2) of which the country of origin is the country or district or locality of that country, the name of which constitutes the appellation of origin of the goods that have given the goods their reputation.

The following should be noted in the development of this provision. Firstly, A.P.

Sergeyev says that a designation must be associated by consumers with a certain place of origin. "If such associations do not arise, the designation, even including the name of the geographical object, cannot be declared as an appellation of origin of goods" [56, p. 607]. [56, c. 607]. In addition, the names of geographical objects are associated by the public with certain properties of goods that are produced in this area. In this case, as stated in the work of V.A. Dozortsev, "special properties should have a stable, stable and known character" [57, p. 273] [57, c. 273]

At the same time, this issue is not clearly resolved in either Belarusian or Russian legislation. In the practice of Rospatent there were cases of refusal to register as an appellation of origin of goods a designation due to lack of fame, in particular, such designation as "Essentuki Healing" [58]. However, due to the lack of uniform application of this provision, it is criticised. In particular, M.A. Saltykov believes that it is necessary to abolish the requirement of object fame, and the term "appellation of origin of goods" should be replaced by the term "geographical indication" [12, p. 8]. [12, c. 8].

L.L.Kiriy and S.A.Gorlenko on this issue substantiate the need to introduce along with the appellation of origin of goods also geographical indication as an independent object of intellectual property (similar to the Geneva Act) [59]. The Ukrainian researcher O.O.Kovalchuk writes about the same in his dissertation work [60, p. 6].

At the same time, in our opinion, the introduction of an additional object "geographical indication" with granting it legal protection in the registration procedure along with the appellation of origin of goods under the existing definition will lead to "overlapping" of the criteria for granting legal protection to each of the objects, and the presence of the signs "exclusively", "mainly", "essentially", which are not clearly defined at the legislative level, will cause additional difficulties in the registration procedure of such designations. In addition, the practice of Ukraine on this issue can be cited as an example. Despite the presence in the legislation of two objects similar in definition to the appellation of origin and geographical indication and protected by the registration procedure, in practice in Ukraine out of 42 qualified designations of origin of goods only 1 geographical indication related to Georgia - vodka from grape pomace "Chacha" has been registered [61].

In addition, Article 9 of the Geneva Act states that Contracting Parties which do not distinguish in their national or regional legislation between an appellation of origin and a geographical indication are not required to introduce such a distinction in their national or regional legislation, provided that that legislation treats registered appellations of origin as registered geographical indications.

In connection with the above, we believe that for the purposes of uniformity of terminology, the concept of "geographical indication" within the meaning of Regulation No. 1151/2012 and the Geneva Act may be included in the concept of "appellation of origin of goods" in its most general sense, which is used in the EAEU states, based on the same scope of legal protection and in order to avoid terminological confusion. At the same time, this definition proposes to exclude the requirement of mandatory familiarity of the designation.

Trademarks

Protection of geographical indications by means of trade marks, both individual and collective, as well as certification marks, is common in common law countries. At the same time, this method of protection is also possible in the countries of the Romano-Germanic system of law, despite the general provisions of the legislation on the prohibition of registration as trademarks of designations of the geographical place of origin of goods.

Thus, in many foreign countries the practice of registering collective marks for individualisation of the designation of the geographical place of origin is widespread. In particular, such practice is applied in the EU both at the level of the Union itself and at the level of individual states. Thus, EU Regulation No. 207/2009 of 26 February 2009. "On the Community trade mark, Article 66(2) provides that collective marks may consist of geographical indications, which is an exception to the general rule that designations of geographical place of origin cannot be registered as trade marks.

The peculiarity of such collective marks is that their registration does not entitle the owner to prohibit the use of such geographical indications by third parties, if this use is lawful, i.e. the goods produced by these persons originate from the territory of this geographical object [62].

A similar rule is contained in paragraph 99 of the Trade Marks Act of the Federal Republic of Germany. For example, the names of such foodstuffs as "Dresdner Christstollen" ("Dresden Christmas cakes") and "Niimberger Lebkuchen" ("Nuremberg gingerbread") are registered as collective marks in Germany [63].

The most typical example of legal regulation under certification mark legislation is usually cited as a Belgian law that established the right of the King to appoint one or more authorised bodies to certify the conformity of goods marked with a geographical indication with the requirements set out in the ordinance recognizing the geographical indication as a protected subject. Such confirmation is carried out by issuing a certificate to the producer of the goods concerned. At the same time, the king also establishes the conditions to be met by these bodies, the guarantees they must provide in order to obtain authorisation for certification, as well as the amount of fees they can receive for issuing certificates of origin [26, p. 399].

The use of individual trademarks is also possible, but only if this designation is associated not with a geographical location, but with a specific production origin of the product, i.e. has acquired the so-called "secondary meaning" [38, c. 15]. This follows from the provision of paragraph C (1) of Article b-quinques of the Paris Convention, according to which "in order to determine whether a mark can be the subject of protection, it is necessary to take into account all the factual circumstances, especially the duration of use of the mark" [30]. [30]. What is at issue here is the acquisition of distinctiveness by the mark.

It is necessary to dwell on this issue in more detail. There is no legal definition of distinctiveness in international documents. At the same time, distinctiveness is usually understood as a certain set of external features of a sign, which allows it to be easily recognised, remembered, recognised when marking goods [23, p. 26]. According to N.Y. Medvedev, "a designation is considered to have acquired distinctiveness as a result of use, if a significant part of consumers perceives it as a means of individualisation of goods or services. It is not required that the consumer associates this designation with a particular manufacturer" [17, p. 8]. [17, c. 8]. M.N. Zubkova gives the following definition of distinctiveness: "Distinctiveness is the ability of a sign to give products (services) features of individuality, uniqueness and originality, to make products (services) for consumers recognisable and memorable among other homogeneous products (services)" [21, p. 15]. [21, c. 15].

Distinctiveness must be both absolute - the trademark must individualise the goods of a given manufacturer by itself, regardless of the presence of other trademarks or trademark applications, and relative - the trademark must not be identical or confusingly similar to another trademark. Absolute grounds for refusal without comparison with other objects of third party rights allow to assess the essence (the so-called "intrinsic value") of the designation applied for registration, its ability to perform the functions of a trademark, and, first of all, the main - individualising function. "Relative" grounds for refusal should answer the question: in case of its registration as a trademark, will the claimed designation violate the rights of third parties to other objects, including registered trademarks? In this case, the evaluation of the designation is carried out on the basis of comparison with other objects of third party rights. [64, c. 48].

However, in order to register a trade mark, in addition to the distinctiveness of the designation, it is necessary that there is no need for its free use.

In order to be able to register a geographical indication as a trade mark (its protected element), such indication must represent or otherwise reflect the true place of origin of goods. Otherwise, such a trademark cannot be registered. At the same time, designations which, although they include the name of the geographical object, in fact, cannot be perceived as trademarks with the designation of the geographical place of origin of goods, due to the unreality of their connection with the geographical object, appear as fantasy ones. Such designations can be registered as trademarks in the case when they are not perceived in the consumer's mind as a designation of the place of origin of goods or the tradition of designations in this area provides for the use of geographical designations as a means of individualisation, and in everyday life the product and the geographical object are not associated with each other [51, p. 144].

The acquisition of distinctiveness by a trademark will take place when the use by an enterprise of the designation of the geographical place of origin of a product in the labelling of its goods forms over time such a link between the respective reputation of the goods and that designation that in the minds of consumers the presence of such a geographical designation on certain types of goods will cause an association not so much with the geographical place, but directly with the goods themselves.

It should be noted that in the Russian Federation the Order of Rospatent No. 39 dated 23 March 2001 "On Approval of Recommendations on Certain Issues of Examination of Claimed Designations", Section 2.4 of which is devoted to the peculiarities of examination of designations consisting of or including geographical names, is in force on this issue. In accordance with this Order, two types of such designations are distinguished:

1. designations which are claimed in respect of goods whose characteristics are related to geographical origin. In this case, the geographical name indicates the place of production or marketing of the goods, the location of the manufacturer of the goods and the

geographical origin of the goods (i.e. in this case, it is an indication of the origin of the goods);

2.	designations that are claimed for goods whose characteristics are not related to geographical origin. In this case, the geographical name indicates only the place of production or marketing of the goods and the location of the manufacturer.

In the case of the first type of designation, according to this Order, it is not advisable to grant it legal protection even if the applicant provides convincing evidence that the consumer perceives the designation as the trademark of the manufacturer.

This approach is explained by the fact that a geographical name indicating the geographical origin of the goods should be free for use by different manufacturers producing goods, the quality, reputation and other characteristics of which are related to the peculiarities of the place of production of the goods, its natural conditions. The designation "CASPII" for the product "black caviar" is given as an example. Even if the applicant proves that the designation is perceived by the consumer as the trademark of the producer, it should still be possible for the various producers of black caviar in the region to use this designation indicating the place of production of the product "caviar" to characterise the black caviar they produce, which has a reputation associated with the Caspian Sea.

If we are talking about the second type of designations, then, depending on the amount of information contained in the sources of information, these designations can be conditionally divided into two groups:

- which are well-known geographical names that can be perceived as the location of the manufacturer;

- which are obscure names that are unlikely to be perceived as the location of the manufacturer.

If a designation belongs to the first group, it is not advisable to grant legal protection to it, except for the case when the applicant has submitted materials confirming that the consumer perceived the claimed designation before the date of filing of the application as a designation of the manufacturer's goods.

If the designation belongs to the second group, it may be granted legal protection [65].

Another classification of geographical indications that may be registered as trademarks (their protected elements) is reflected in the authoritative WIPO publication "Introduction to Intellectual Property".

According to this classification, distinctive, i.e., possessing distinctiveness, are:

а) obscure designations;

б) references to areas where no one would expect certain goods to be produced;

в) known designations if there are no other industrialists or traders in the same field of activity and there is no potential for future competitors to establish themselves there;

г)	a designation which, through long and intensive use, is associated with a certain enterprise to such an extent that it becomes distinctive as a trademark for it, even if competitors already exist or assert themselves in the future [41, p. 186].

Thus, if we analyse the above two classifications, we can identify two main features that determine the possibility of registration of designations of the geographical place of origin of goods as a trademark:

1.	objective - the characteristics of a commodity are related to its geographical origin;

2.	subjective - a significant proportion of consumers associate the designation as geographical.

In this regard, 3 different combinations of these attributes can be distinguished:

1.	Regardless of the presence of a subjective attribute, there is an objective attribute. In this case, registration of such a designation should be refused, since there is a need for its free use.

2.	Subjective sign is present, objective sign is absent. Registration is possible in two cases:

a)	if there is no production of homogeneous goods in the area and there is no potential for future production of such goods;

б)	if the designation has acquired a so-called "secondary meaning".

According to M.N. Sokolova, the fact of the absence of production of homogeneous goods and the potential for the future production of such goods should be confirmed by an authorised territorial body, which can be, for example, the executive authority of an administrative-territorial unit [11, p. 19].

3.	Subjective and objective signs are missing. These are little-known geographical indications, and the characteristics of the goods are not related to their geographical origin. The designation may be registered as a trade mark.

This thesis is also reflected in the publications of Russian specialists in the field of intellectual property, who refer to the practice of registration of trademarks in the Patent Office of the Russian Federation [24, p. 29].

Thus, the condition for granting a geographical designation legal protection as an indication of origin of goods is that the properties of goods are conditioned to any extent by their geographical origin (an objective criterion). At the same time, in order to protect an indication of origin of goods, it is not necessary that this designation be known to consumers.

The condition for legal protection of a designation as a geographical indication within the meaning of the TRIPS Agreement is that the properties of goods are essentially attributable to their origin. The legal protection of such a designation does not require its registration, which is where the term differs from the concept of "geographical indication" within the meaning of Regulation 1151/2012 and the Geneva Act.

At the same time, in order for a designation to receive legal protection as an appellation of origin of goods, the properties of the goods must be conditioned by the place of their origin exclusively or mainly. At the same time, the appellation of origin can be considered in a narrow sense, which is enshrined in the current version of the Lisbon Agreement and implies a rather strict link between the properties of goods and the geographical environment, as well as in a broader sense, which combines the concepts of "appellation of origin" (PDO) and "geographical indication" (PGI) from Regulation 1151/2012 and provides the possibility of registration as an appellation of origin for a wider list of designations. The first definition is classical, the second one is used, in particular, in the legislation of the EAEU member states. At the same time, in our opinion, its definition requires the exclusion of the requirement on the fame of the designation.

The designation of the geographical place of origin of goods may be legally protected by registration of a collective or certification mark. Registration of an individual mark is possible when the applied-for designation has acquired a distinctive character (so-called "secondary meaning"). To identify this, it is necessary to determine the combination of objective (presence of certain properties determined by the place of origin of goods) and subjective (perception of the designation as geographical) criteria. If the objective criterion is present, registration of such a designation as a trade mark is excluded.

CHAPTER 3

**PECULIARITIES OF THE SUBJECT COMPOSITION AND RIGHTS TO
GEOGRAPHICAL INDICATIONS**

As noted earlier, the specificity of designations of the geographical place of origin of goods lies in the fact that the right to use them, as a general rule, should be free for use by all persons producing goods in the territory of the designated geographical object. This determines certain specificity of the rights to use the designation of origin of goods, geographical indication and appellation of origin of goods.

Thus, one of the most important characteristics of an intellectual property object is an exclusive right. In this case, the content of the exclusive right usually includes the powers granted to its owner to use a certain intellectual property object alone, to authorise and prohibit the use of the object by third parties (who are not in a legal relationship with the owner of the right).

If it is an indication of origin of goods or a geographical indication in the sense of the TRIPS Agreement, the essence of their legal protection is to prevent the use of false (fake) indications, as well as misleading the consumer as to the real place of origin of goods, which does not relate to the content of the exclusive right.

With respect to the appellation of origin of goods, the person who has the right to use it, as a general rule, has the authority only to use it, and not alone, since the right to use the appellation of origin of goods may be granted to several persons; and also to prohibit its use, but not to any other person, but only to those persons who are not authorised to do so. At the same time, assignment of the right to use the appellation of origin of goods and granting the right to use it on the basis of a licence are not allowed, which indicates that there is also no right of disposal.

In this connection, there are different points of view on the content of the right to use the appellation of origin of goods.

Thus, it is quite common that the right to use the appellation of origin of goods is not exclusive [66, p. 295]. At the same time, according to S.P. Grishaev, the exclusive right to use the appellation of origin of goods is in the sense that a person who is not registered as the owner of the right to use the appellation of origin of goods and does not have the relevant certificate, is not entitled to use such a registered designation, even if the true place of origin of goods is indicated. Thus, if perfume, the place of origin of which will be indicated the city of Paris, such a name may mislead, if it is not the French capital, with which the consumer is associated with associations in relation to the high quality of perfume, and a small town in the United States (as is known, many settlements in the U.S. have names of famous European cities). [67, c. 234].

It should be noted that in this case the author uses the term appellation of origin of goods, however, based on the content of protection, it should be an indication of the origin of goods.

A similar point of view is held by E.P. Gavrilov [68, p. 154].

According to N.M. Frolova, this right is a "truncated", "weakened" exclusive right [69,

p. 79]. In another publication the same author suggests the name "limited exclusive rights" [70, p. 309] [70, c. 309].

There are other points of view on this right. Thus, N.V. Chang considers it a right of a special kind or sui generis, which has no analogues in the sphere of exclusive rights [15, p. 20]. As a collective right to use the appellation of origin of goods is considered by other Russian specialists [50, p. 5; 26]. At the same time, such a right is often possessed by a single subject. Zykov SV. refers this right to "atypical", because the principles of absoluteness, negotiability, as well as the term of validity of rights, characteristic of the exclusive right, are undermined [71, p. 67].

The above is also true for a geographical indication within the meaning of Regulation 1151/2012 and the Geneva Act. Thus, from the point of view of the German jurist F. Schwarz, which he expresses in his work "Protection of Geographical Indications", a geographical indication lacks the function of individual exclusivity characteristic of intangible objects, since it is usually owned by several producers. Geographical indications are collective designations and do not confer sole exclusivity, as it is not granted to other producers from the same region. Based on the analysis of different points of view, the author comes to the opinion that in this case we can talk about an intangible property right with a limited function of exclusivity [72, p. 3-4].

Despite this diversity of existing opinions, two indisputable points can be emphasised with regard to the right to use the appellation of origin of goods:

1.		the said right cannot be recognised as an exclusive right in its classical sense due to the existence of the two exceptions mentioned above;

2.		the said right cannot be completely separated from the category of "exclusive right", as it contains the features of an exclusive right.

On the basis of the above, we should agree with the interpretation of this right as a "truncated" or "limited" exclusive right, which will better reflect its essence.

At the same time, it is possible to assume the existence of such a right, which is labelled in some publications as "the right to the appellation of origin of goods". The existence of this right can be "discovered" in a situation when all the certificates issued for the right to use the appellation of origin of goods cease to be valid. At the same time, the legislation of many states, in particular, Article 1536 of the Civil Code of the Russian Federation, does not contain provisions on the termination of legal protection of the appellation of origin of goods. On this issue L.L. Kiriy notes that many appellations of origin registered in Russia do not have users, i.e. after 10 years after registration the holders of certificates do not extend the term of validity of the exclusive right to the appellation. As an example, such names as "Zhostovo", "Fedoskino", "Krasnoselskaya skan", "Ryazan Uzory", etc. are given. [16, c. 19]. Consequently, in this situation there is no right to use the appellation of origin of goods, but the name itself continues to be protected as an object of intellectual property, which implies the existence of some right to it.

There are several points of view on this issue. Thus, V.V. Kolesnikova V.V. distinguishes between the right to use the appellation of origin of goods, which she defines as exclusive with a limited nature, and the right to the appellation of origin of goods, which she considers as absolute and belonging to the state [73, p. 21]. The same opinion is held by A.P. Rabets [19, p. 113].

N.V. Chang, although does not directly call this right, but expresses the point of view that the users of the appellation of origin of goods have only permission from the relevant state body to use the geographical designation, if their goods are characterised by special qualities and are produced in the place that gave its name to the geographical designation placed on their goods [15, p. 19].

In practice, this approach is implemented in the legislation of Mexico, which enshrines a provision according to which the owner of all Mexican appellations of origin is the government of that country. And authorisation for their use by interested parties on behalf of the government is granted by the Secretariat of Trade and Industrial Development [74].

This approach can be extended to geographical indications, which are a more general concept. Thus, proposals to recognise the state as the owner of national geographical indications were made by M.I. Arkhipova [14, p. 17] and O.O. Kovalchuk [75, p. 15] in their thesis. G.M. Dmitrichenko points out that the basis for the registration of geographical indications (according to Ukrainian legislation) is public interest, and the right to a registered geographical indication is not a private right [76, p. 11]. At the same time, the author proposes to fix the provisions on the belonging of geographical indications to the Ukrainian people [76, p. 14].

Another approach to this issue is the opinion that the right to the appellation of origin is a collective right and belongs to all producers of goods who have the right to use it [77, p. 158]. However, in this case, the most common situation when the right to use the appellation of origin of goods belongs to a single person, the producer of goods with certain properties, remains uncovered.

Finally, there is a third point of view, according to which the right to the appellation of origin has no individually determined owner at all - a subject endowed with a monopoly right to this object of industrial property [78]. However, the existence of an object and a subjective right to it should also provide for the presence of a certain subject, because otherwise there is no point in talking about a certain right.

We believe that based on the very essence of the appellation of origin of goods as a designation of a certain geographical object, which is the property of one or another state (several states, if it is an international name), we can conclude that it is more appropriate to recognise the right to the appellation of origin of goods as an absolute right for a state (several states). The same applies to geographical indications. At the same time, the procedure of granting the right to use the name may be considered as granting on behalf of the state the authorisation to use it.

This issue is not only of theoretical but also of considerable practical importance. Thus, in accordance with Article 5 of the Lisbon Agreement, the registration of the appellation of origin is carried out on behalf of any natural persons, as well as legal entities in the broad sense of the word ("legal entities"), public or private, which, according to their national legislation, have the right to use such appellations.

In this connection, in many legislations, the applicant can only be the producer of goods with special properties, who in the case of registration of the appellation of origin is granted the limited exclusive right to use the appellation discussed above.

In the European Union, there is a close link between producers of goods who must form an association (in the form of an association or consortium) to register and protect geographical indications or appellations of origin, both within the EU and abroad. Thus, the circle of persons who can register appellations of origin is significantly limited at the EU level.

At the same time, two groups of subjects of the right to use the appellation of origin of goods can be distinguished:

1.   entities that have registered the appellation of origin of goods and obtained the right to use it (the so-called "primary" users);

2.   subjects who have obtained the right to use an already registered appellation of origin of goods (so-called "secondary" users).

This classification is also widespread in the scientific literature on the issues of legal protection of means of individualisation, and in particular, the appellation of origin of goods. Thus, O. A. Gorodov calls the first group of subjects of the "first turn", and the second group - subjects of the "subsequent turns" [79, p.47].

It is important that there are no differences between "primary" and "secondary" users in the content of the right to use the appellation of origin of goods. At the same time, the existence of a registered appellation simplifies the possibility of obtaining the right to use it.

At the same time, in some foreign countries the range of entities entitled to apply for registration of the appellation of origin is much wider than in Belarusian or Russian legislation.

Thus, in accordance with the Law of Ukraine of 16 June 1999 "On Protection of Rights to Indication of Origin of Goods" the right to register a qualified indication of origin of goods have:

- a person or group of persons who, in the geographical location claimed, produces a good whose special characteristics, particular qualities, reputation or other attributes are associated with that geographical location.

- consumer associations;

- Institutions that are directly related to the production or study of the products, articles, processes or geographical locations concerned.

However, the right to use such an indication is available, subject to registration of that right, to producers who, in the geographical location indicated in the register, produce a product with the above-mentioned characteristics [80].

In accordance with the Law of Georgia "On Appellations of Origin and Geographical Indications of Goods", which entered into force on 1 November 1999, the applicant of the appellation of origin of goods may be a natural person or a legal entity, a public authority or a legal entity of public law, as well as a voluntary association of entrepreneurs of any organisational and legal form. At the same time, these subjects may both register these objects and acquire the right to use them, and perform only one of these two actions [81].

Thus, the analysis of the above-mentioned provisions of the legislation allows us to conclude that an application for registration of the appellation of origin of goods may be filed not only by its producers, but also by other subjects, in particular, by state organisations and institutions, which are in any way connected with the production or study of the relevant goods, and which exercise the powers of the state as the owner of the right to the appellation of origin of goods.

We believe that such norms on the subject composition are more in line with the essence of the appellation of origin of goods as the property of a particular state.

By its legal regime with the appellation of origin of goods is also similar to the collective mark. The peculiarity of this legal regime is that even in the case of registration of a collective mark, users have a narrower ("truncated") exclusive right to use the designation [82, p. 16]. Firstly, the user has no right to assign such a designation or transfer the right to use it under a licence agreement, and secondly, the user has no right to prohibit the use of these objects by any other persons authorised to do so.

At the same time, the differences between these objects lie, first of all, in the fact that the registration of a collective mark does not require confirmation by the state of the special properties of goods, which is the case with the registration of the appellation of origin of goods. In addition, as a general rule, control over the use of the appellation of origin is exercised by the state authorities authorised to do so, whereas in the case of registration of a collective mark, control is exercised by the association itself, i.e. by the owner of the collective mark.

The subject of the right to a collective mark is an association of legal entities, which in practice is most often an association or union. The subjects of the right to a trade mark are most often legal entities and citizens.

At the same time, according to M.N. Sokol his "right to dispose of a "geographical" trademark by its owner has limitations: the owner of a "geographical" trademark can alienate such trademark or grant a licence for its use to another economic entity that is located in the given geographical object or in close proximity to it (in accordance with the objective reasons that existed when granting the exclusive right to such a designation)". In this regard, the author concludes that the position of the owner of such a trademark is less strong compared to the owners of other trademarks [11, p. 22].

We believe that this statement is only partially true. As discussed in the previous chapter, a trade mark representing or containing the designation of a geographical place of origin may be granted legal protection in three cases. However, only one of these cases involves the association of consumers with a geographical place - if there is no production of homogeneous goods in the area and no potential for future production of such goods. The other two cases refer either to a little-known designation or to a designation that has acquired a so-called "secondary meaning". "secondary meaning".

Resolution of conflicts between appellation of origin and trade marks

Of great scientific and practical interest is the issue of the collision of a trade mark with the appellation of origin of goods. Recently in the world practice the principle of priority of the appellation of origin over the trade mark, enshrined in the Lisbon Agreement, was used. Thus, in particular, in the lawsuit between the company "Pilsen" (plaintiff) and the Italian firm "Industrie Poretti SpA" (defendant), the Supreme Court of Italy established that "if the defendant uses a designation that is similar to the appellation of origin registered in the name of the plaintiff, and which is the only element of the plaintiff's trademark, then when assessing these actions should be guided by the norms of the law on appellations of origin, not the law on trademarks [20, p. 246].

The most famous example of a clash between a trademark and an appellation of origin is the dispute between the owner of the trademark "Budweiser", the American beer producer Anheuser-Bush, and the Czech brewery Budejovicky Budvar, which had the right to use the appellation of origin "Cesky Budejovicky Budvar". The German and English translations of these designations contain the word "Budweiser". Both designations are respectively used in relation to the same goods - beer. The battle was fought in courts in more than 100 countries, with success alternating between one side and the other. Anheuser-Bush is believed to be the company that prompted the US to initiate proceedings at the WTO to assess the legality of Europe's system of special protection for appellations of origin, arguing that trade marks take precedence over appellations of origin. The WTO ruled that member countries can introduce limited exceptions to the rights granted to trademarks, and ruled against the U.S., indicating that both systems of protection of these objects can coexist. [83, c. 24].

It should be noted, however, that the TRIPS Agreement, in Article 16(1), contains a provision on the exclusive right of the trade mark owner not to authorise third parties, without its consent, to use identical or similar signs for homogeneous goods where such use would give rise to a likelihood of confusion. It is noted that these rights are without prejudice to any existing rights arising earlier.

At the same time, as noted above, Article 24 of TRIPS provides for enhanced protection of certain geographical indications (for wines and spirits). Article 24(5) of the TRIPS Agreement states that where a trade mark application or registration has been made in good faith, measures to protect such indications shall not prejudice the registrability or validity of the trade mark.

On 15 March 2005, a decision of the WTO Dispute Settlement Board (WT/DS174/R) was handed down, which was based on the rules of Article 16 of the TRIPS Agreement. This decision led to a radical revision of the system of protection of the appellation of origin in the European Community and was embodied first in Regulation No. 510/2006 and then in Regulation No. 1151/2012 [84].

According to Article 6 (4) of Regulation No. 1151/2012, a protected appellation of origin and a protected geographical indication may not be registered if, because of the reputation and fame of the trade mark and the length of time it has been in use, the registration is likely to mislead the consumer as to the true origin of the goods.

Thus, the priority between trademarks and appellations of origin is determined by the date of their registration ("first in time, first in right"). In addition, it is necessary to have a certain reputation and fame of the trademark.

It should be noted that the second paragraph of paragraph 2 of Article 1535 of the Civil Code of the Russian Federation, along with similar general grounds, contains a special ground for invalidating the registration of the appellation of origin of goods. Thus, if the use of the appellation of origin of goods is capable of misleading the consumer as to the goods or its manufacturer due to the presence of a trademark having an earlier priority, the granting of legal protection to the said appellation may be challenged and declared invalid within five years from the date of publication of information on the state registration of the appellation of origin of goods in the official gazette.

Paragraph 2 of Article 39 of the Law of the Republic of Kazakhstan of 26 July 1999 "On trademarks, service marks and appellations of origin of goods" contains a similar wording. At the same time, the opposing trademark must have a wide fame in the Republic of Kazakhstan, acquired as a result of active use [85].

At the same time, the current wording of the Russian Civil Code has been criticised by a number of researchers. In particular, it is noted that it uses a narrower concept of "misrepresentation" in comparison with the term "likelihood of confusion" established by the TRIPS Agreement, and also refers to an already registered appellation of origin of goods, excluding the application for registration of the appellation of origin of goods [86].

The above allows us to draw the following conclusions. The rights to use the indication of origin of goods, geographical indication and appellation of origin of goods have their own specificity in contrast to other objects of industrial property. As for the right to use the appellation of origin of goods, the analysis of various points of view on this issue allows us to conclude that this right cannot be called fully exclusive in its classical sense, but, at the same time, it contains certain features of an exclusive right.

In addition to the right to use the appellation of origin of goods, it is also possible to distinguish the right to the appellation of origin of goods, as well as the right to geographical indication, which it is reasonable to recognise as an absolute right for the state.

The legal regime of the collective mark is similar in nature to the right to use the appellation of origin of goods. However, the difference lies in the fact that the registration of a collective mark does not require confirmation by the state of the special properties of the goods and control over their existence.

In some cases, the right to dispose of a trade mark that represents or contains a geographical indication as a protected element may be restricted due to the possibility of misleading consumers as to the place of origin (production) of goods.

In the case of a clash between a trade mark and an appellation of origin, the priority is currently determined by the date of registration of the respective objects, but only if there is a certain reputation and fame of the trade mark.

CONCLUSION

Geographical indications can rightly be called historically the first means of individualisation of goods, which began to be used before our era and served as an indicator that the goods had certain properties caused by geographical origin. However, at the first stage their legal protection was fragmentary and did not contribute to the prevention of unfair competition in this area.

In connection with the evolution of means of individualisation from general to more specific, the first legislative acts on the protection of trademarks appear, while any geographical indications are not considered as an independent object of industrial property. The Paris Convention of 1883 mentions the concept of "indication of origin" in connection with the prohibition of the use of false indications of origin. Shortly thereafter, designations of origin were for the first time made the subject of an international treaty, the Madrid Agreement of 1891. In 1911, the indication of origin was included in the list of industrial property objects protected by the Paris Convention. This marks the beginning of the second stage in the protection of geographical indications.

Since the 20s of the 20th century in France and other countries of mainly Southern Europe, as well as some other states, a new object of industrial property has been legislated - the appellation of place of origin of goods, which is a designation of goods, the special properties of which are conditioned exclusively or mainly by the geographical environment. In 1925 the appellation of origin was included in the list of industrial property objects in the Paris Convention, which was the beginning of the third stage in the protection of geographical designations. The development of its legal protection leads in 1957 to the conclusion of the Lisbon Agreement, which created an international system of registration of appellations of origin, which, however, has not been widely spread in the world.

With the deepening of European integration processes, there is a need for common approaches to this issue and the creation of a regional system of legal protection of geographical indications, which was reflected in Regulation 2081/92. This document, in addition to the protected appellation of origin, introduced legal protection of another object, the protected geographical indication, with less stringent protection criteria.

In the United States and other "common" law countries, the above terms are not legally recognised, and protection for geographical indications is granted mainly in the context of certification marks, as well as collective marks.

At present, three main systems of granting legal protection to geographical indications can be distinguished in the world: "German" (protection is exercised mainly through indications of origin), "French" (along with indications of origin, appellations of origin are protected), "American" (protection is exercised on the basis of legislation on countering unfair competition and legislation on trademarks and certification marks).

The diversity of forms of legal protection of geographical indications has led WIPO to endeavour, since the mid-1970s, to develop an international treaty that would define uniform criteria for their protection. However, to date no such treaty has been concluded. However, within the framework of the WTO, the TRIPS Agreement has attempted to define minimum standards for the protection of geographical indications within the term "geographical indication", which is substantively different from the similar term in Regulation 1151/2012. At the same time, the enshrinement of such a term in an international agreement indicates the beginning of the fourth stage of geographical indication protection.

On 20 May 2015, at the WIPO Diplomatic Conference, 11 States signed the Geneva Act, which is an amended Lisbon Agreement granting registration protection to geographical indications in addition to appellations of origin.

Thus, indications of origin are currently the most widely protected in the world, with the scope of their legal protection being the prohibition of the use of false and misleading indications. An analysis of various points of view allows us to conclude that indications of origin include geographical indications for goods whose properties are to a certain extent determined by their geographical origin (objective criterion). It does not matter whether the consumer associates this designation as a geographical designation (subjective criterion). At the same time, the subjective criterion is necessary for the legal protection of designations of origin against misleading designations under the Madrid Agreement.

The scope of protection for indications of origin is the same as for geographical indications within the meaning of the TRIPS Agreement, with the exception of wines and spirits, for which a legal regime similar to appellations of origin is established. At the same time, the objective criterion for geographical indications must be expressed to a substantial degree (i.e., the properties of the goods must have a significant link to the geographical origin). However, the TRIPS Agreement does not provide for mandatory registration of geographical indications, which distinguishes them from the similar term in the Geneva Act.

With regard to the appellation of origin of goods, it should be noted that its original definition, enshrined in the current version of the Lisbon Agreement, assumes the connection of goods with the concept of "geographical environment", which creates a very strict framework for its protection. At the same time, the theory, as well as the legislation of some states and international acts (the Treaty on the EAEU) provide for a broader definition of the appellation of origin of goods, which combines the concepts of "appellation of origin" and "geographical indication" from the Geneva Act and provides an opportunity for registration as an appellation of origin of goods to a wider list of designations. At the same time, the said definition provides for the renown of the designation as a mandatory criterion. Since in the Russian practice and in the practice of other states with such definition there are no uniform requirements for confirmation of such fame, and the concept of "geographical indication" does not provide for such criterion, it is proposed to delete this requirement.

Legal protection of a geographical designation may be exercised through registration of a collective or certification mark. Registration of an individual mark is possible when the claimed geographical designation is of a fantasy nature and is not perceived as a designation of the place of origin of goods, or has acquired a so-called "secondary meaning" in the process of use. In order to determine the acquisition of such meaning it is necessary to establish the presence of objective and subjective criteria, various combinations of which determine the possibility of granting the designation legal protection as a trade mark. In any case, if there is an objective criterion, registration of such a designation is excluded.

With regard to the content of designation of origin and geographical indication rights within the meaning of the TRIPS Agreement, it should be emphasised that they are not exclusive rights, as the essence of their legal protection is to prevent the use of false or misleading indications.

As for the right to use the appellation of origin of goods, there are different points of view. At the same time, it is common that the said right cannot be called fully exclusive in its classical sense, but, at the same time, it contains certain features of an exclusive right. The same applies to a geographical indication within the meaning of the Geneva Act.

Along with the right to use the appellation of origin of goods, one can also distinguish the right to the appellation of origin of goods. The analysis of this right shows that due to the special significance of this object it is advisable to recognise it as an absolute right for the state.

The legal regime of a collective mark is similar to the right to use the appellation of origin of goods. At the same time, the registration of a collective mark does not require the state to confirm the special properties of goods. When using a collective mark, the state does not exercise control over their existence.

A geographical indication registered as a trade mark may, in some cases, result in a restriction on the disposition of such trade mark due to the possibility of misleading consumers.

The problem of collision between a trade mark and an appellation of origin is topical. At the same time, according to the international documents currently in force (in particular, the TRIPS Agreement), the priority is determined by the date of registration of the respective objects. At the same time, a trademark must have a certain reputation and fame.

We believe that in the near future the issues of legal protection of geographical indications will continue to be a topical area of research.

LIST OF SOURCES USED

1. Geographical Indications. A Review of Proposals at the TRIPS Council: Extending Article 23 to Products other than Wines and Spirites / By Dr Dwijen Rangnekar *I I* Intellectual Property Rigths aim Sustainable Development, June 2003.-52 p.

2. Kickler, H. Die Geschichte des Schutzes geographischer Herkunftsangaben in Deutschland *I* H. Kickler *I I* Mohr Siebeck Tubingen, 2012. - 503 c.

3. Lackert, C. Geographical indications: past, present and future / Clark Lackert *And* Ninis, Howes, Collison, Hansen & Lackert. June 2000

4. O'Connor, B. The Law of Geographical Indications / Bernard O'Connor - Cameron May, 2004. - 500 c.

5. Spuhler, O. Das System des intemationalen und supranationalen Schutzes von Marken und geographischen Herkunftsangaben / von Oliver Spuhler. - Berlin: Duncker und Humboldt, 2000. - 381 c.

6. Tytskaya, G.I. Legal protection of trademarks, trade names, indications and appellations of origin of goods in capital and developing countries / G.I. Tytskaya, I.E. Mamiofa, V.Y. Motyleva. - M.: VNIIPI, 1985. - 71 c.

7. Grigoriev, AN. Geographical indications : problems of legal protection at the national and international levels : autoref. dis. ... Candidate of Jurisprudence: 12.00.03 / AN. Grigoriev - M., 1995. - 23 c.

8. Gorlenko, S.A. Legal protection of appellations of origin of goods / S.A. Gorlenko. - 4th ed., revision and supplement. - M. : INIC Rospatent, 2004.-116 p.

9. Gavrilov, EL. Practice of protection of appellations of origin of goods: what has changed? / E.P. Gavrilov, E.A. Danilina // Patents and Licences - 2006. - № 1-2.

10. Kitaysky, V.E. Appellations of origin of goods: the discussion continues / V.E. Kitaysky // Patents and licences - 2006. - №3. C. 20-24

11. Sokolova, M.N. Legal problems of protection of means of individualisation of goods containing geographical designations: autoref. dis.... Candidate of Juridical Sciences: 12.00.03 / M.N.Sokolova. - M., 2002. - 28 c.

12. Saltykov, M.A. Legal protection of the appellation of origin of goods as one of the objects of intellectual rights: autoref. dis. ... Candidate of Jurisprudence: 12.00.03 / M.A. Saltykov - Moscow, 2012. - 26 c.

13. Takhirov, G. A. Improvement of legal protection of geographical indications in the Republic of Tajikistan : author's dissertation. Candidate of Juridical Sciences: 12.00.03 / G.A. Takhirov - M., 2004. - 24 c.

14. Arkhipova, M.I.. Civic-legal protection of geographical values in Ukraine : author's thesis for the degree of candidate of jurisprudence : speciality. 12.00.03 "Civil law and civil process; criminal law; international private law / M1.Arkhipova. - Kyiv. - 2006. - 21c.

15. Chang, N.V. Geographical indications as objects of legal protection in Vietnam and in Russia: author's thesis. Candidate of Jurisprudence: 12.00.03 / V.CH. Nguyen.- M., 2003. - 33 c.

16. Kyrii, L.L. Geographical indications as a means of economic development of regions / L.L. Kyrii *And* Patents and Licences - 2013.- № 7.- C. 15-20.

17. Medvedev, N.Y. Protection of trade marks under the legislation of the Russian Federation: autoref. dis. ... Candidate of Juridical Sciences: 12.00.03 / N.Yu.Medvedev. -M., 2008. - 23 c.

18. Sadovskiy P.V. Collisions of the rights to trademarks with the rights to the results of intellectual activity and means of individualisation: : autoref. disc. ... Candidate of Jurisprudence: 12.00.03 / P.V. Sadovsky. - Moscow: RGIIS, 2007.-22 p.

19. Rabets, AL. Legal protection of trademarks in Russia =Legal protection of trademarks in Russia *I* AP.Rabets. - SPb. Yurid. centre press, 2003.-338 p.

20. Melnikov, V.M. Trademarks abroad on the eve of the XXI century / VM. Melnikov. - Moscow: ILC Rospatent, 2002. - 300 c.

21. Zubkova, M.N. Legal regime of the trade mark: the correlation of private and public interests: autoref. diss. ... Candidate of Jurisprudence: 12.00.03 / MN.Zubkova. - Volgograd, 2004. - 19 c.

22. Jermakyan, V.Y. Acquisition of distinctiveness by trademarks / V.Y. Jermakyan *And* Patent Attorney. - 2009. - №3.-C. 17-21.

23. Epstein, ML. Interpretation of the concept of distinctiveness of trade marks in court practice / ML. Epshtein *And* Patents and Licences. - 2009.-№3.-C. 25-31.

24. Rogal, I.V. Geographical indications in trademarks and appellations of origin of goods / I.V. Rogal *And* Patents and Licences-2005.- No. I.- P.27-34.

25. Bakhrenkova, K. Geographical indications at the service of world trade / K. Bakhrenkova *And* Intellectual Property in Belarus. - 2006.-№4.-C. 24-29.

26. Intellectual property law: textbook / IA. Bliznets [et al]; ed. by I.A. Bliznets. - Moscow: Prospect, 2010. - 960 c.

27. O'Connor, T. The EU Need Not Be Isolated on GIs *I* T. O'Connor *II* E.I.P.R. -

2007. - Vol. 29. - № 8. - P. 303-306.

28. .WIPO Intellectual Property Law and Treaties Database (WIPO Lex) *I I* World Intellectual Property Organisation [Electronic resource]. - 2017. - Access mode: http://www.wipo.int/wipolex/en/. - Date of access: 05.10.2017.

29. Madrid Agreement Concerning the International Registration of Marks of 14 April 1891, renegotiated at Stockholm on 14 July 1967 and amended on 28 September 1979. 28 September 1979 // World Intellectual Property Organization [Electronic resource]. -2017 . - Mode of access: http://www.wipo.int/treaties/ru/registration/madrid. - Date of access: 05.10.2017.

30. Paris Convention for the Protection of Industrial Property of 20 March 1883, re adopted at Brussels on 14 December 1900, Washington on 2 June 1911, The Hague on 6 November 1925, London on 2 June 1934, Lisbon on 31 October 1958 and Stockholm on 14 July 1967 and amended on 2 October 1979 // World Intellectual Property Organization [Electronic resource]. - 2017. - Mode of access: http://www.wipo.int/treaties/ru/ip/paris/. - Date of access: 05.10.2017.

31. .Madrid Agreement for the Suppression of False or Misleading Indications of Origin on Goods of 14 April 1891, reprinted, at Washington on 2 June 1911, at The Hague on 6 November 1925, at London on 2 June 1934, and at Lisbon on 31 October 1958 / World Intellectual Property Organization [Electronic resource]. - 2017. - Mode of access: http://www.wipo.int/treaties/ en/ip/madrid/. - Date of access: 05.10.2017.

32. Italy : Law No. 125 of April 10,1954, on the Protection of Appellations of Origin and Typical Appellations of Cheeses / WIPO Intellectual Property Law and Treaties Database (WIPO Lex) *11* World Intellectual Property Organisation [Electronic resource]. - 2017. - Access mode: http://www.wipo.int/wipolex/ en/details.jsp?id=2551. - Date of access: 05.10.2017.

33. Italy : Law No. 1618 of December 7, 1951 Transitional Provisions for the Implementation of Law No. 1068 of November 4, 1950, Establishing Standards for the Area of Production & Characteristics of the Typical Wine Known as Moscato di Pantelleria and of Law No. 1069 of November 4, 1950, Establishing Standards for the Area of Production & Characteristics of the Typical Wines Known as Marsala *I* WIPO Intellectual Property Law and Treaties Database (WIPO Lex) // World Intellectual Property Organization [Electronic resource]. - 2017. - Mode of access: http://www.wipo.int/wipolex/en/. - Date of access: 05.10.2017.

34. Lisbon system *AND* World Intellectual Property Organisation [Electronic resource]. - 2017. - Access mode: http://www.wipo.int/treaties/ru/registration/lisbon/. - Date of access: 05.10.2017.

35. Verordnung (EWG) Nr. 2081/92 des Rates vom 14. Juli 1992 zum Schutz von geographischen Angaben und Ursprungsbezeichnungen für Agrarerzeugnisse und Lebensmittel *11* EUR-Lex [Electronic resource]. - 2017. - Access mode: http://eur-lex.europa.eu/LexUriServ/LexUriServ.do?uri=CELEX:31992R2081:DE:HTML. - Access date: 05.10.2017.

36. Verordnung (EG) Nr. 510/2006 des Rates vom 20. Marz 2006 zum Schutz von

geografischen Angaben und Ursprungsbezeichnungen fur Agrarerzeugnisse und Lebensmittel // EUR-Lex [Electronic resource]. - 2017. - Mode Access: http://eur-lex.europa.eu/legal-content/DE/ALL/?uri=CELEX%3A32006R0510. - Date of access: 05.10.2017.

37. Verordnung (EU) No 1151/2012 des Europaischen Parlament und des Rates vom 21. November 2012 uber Qualitatsregelungen fur Agrarerzeugnisse und Lebensmittel *11* EUR-Lex [Electronic resource]. - 2017. - Access mode: http://eur-lex.europa.eu/legal-content/DE/TXT/?qid=1428350790903&uri= CELEX:32O12R1151 - Date of access: 05.10.2017.

38. Obergfell; E.I. "Markenqualitat aus deutschen Landen"- geographische Herkunftsangabe oder gemeinschaftswidriges Giitezeichen *I* Dr. E.I.Obergfell, Dr. W.Hertel *I I* The European Legal Forum. - 2003. - №3. S. 121-127.

39. Agreement on Trade-Related Aspects of Intellectual Property Rights (TRIPS/TRIPS), concluded in Marrakesh 15.04.1994 *And* ConsultantPlus [Electronic resource] / LLC "Yurspectr". - M., 2017.

40. Diplomatic Conference for the Adoption of a new Act of the Lisbon Agreement for the Protection of Appellations of Origin and their International Registration // World Intellectual Property Organisation [Electronic resource]. - 2017. - Mode of access: http://www.wipo.int/meetings/diplomatic_conferences/2015/en/. Date of access: 05.10.2017.

41. Geneva Act of the Lisbon Agreement on Appellations of Origin and Geographical Indications (adopted 20 May 2015)// World Intellectual Property Organization [Electronic resource]. -2017. -Access mode: http://www.wipo.int/wipolex/ru/ treaties/ text.jsp? file_id=376775. - Date of access: 05.10.2017.

42. Bodenhausen, G. Paris Convention for the Protection of Industrial Property / G. Bodenhausen *I* M.: Progress, 1977. - 377 c.

43. .Introduction to Intellectual Property *And* World Intellectual Property Organisation. 652 c.

44. Maggs, P.B., Sergeev A.P. Intellectual Property. - Moscow: Yurist, 2000. - 400 c.

45. Grigoriev A.N. Criteria of protection of geographical indications / A.N. Grigoriev *I* Intellectual property. - 1995. - № 5-6. - C. 15-19.

46. Brethauer, S. Der Schutz der geographischen Herkunftsangaben *I* C. Brethauer *1 1* Rechtsanwalt Gottingen [Electronic resource]. - 2017. - Access mode: http://www.markenrecht.justlaw.de/geographische-herkunftsangaben.htni - Date of access: 05.10.2017.

47. Grigoriev A. N. Correlation of trade mark and geographical indication. Patents and Licences. 1994, No. 7, pp. 17 - 21.

48. Frequently Asked Questions: Geographical Indications. // WIPO. World Intellectual Property Organisation [Electronic resource]. -2017. -Access mode : http://www.wipo.int/geo_indications/ru/faq_geographicalindications.html Date of access: 05.10.2017.

49. .Lisbon Agreement Ent for the Protection of Appellations of Origin and their International Registration of 31 October 1958, renegotiated at Stockholm on 14 July 1967

and amended on 28 September 1979 // World Intellectual Property Organization [Electronic resource]. - 2017. - Mode of access:
http://www.wipo.int/lisbon/en/legal_texts/Hsbon_agreement.html. - Date of access: 05.10.2017.

50. Ionova, O.V. International agreements on the protection of appellations of origin and designations of origin of goods / State Patent Office of the USSR. - M.: VNIIPI, 1992. - 40 c.

51. Shtoppel, V. Protection of geographical indications of origin and appellations of origin of goods / V. Shtoppel *And* Issues of intellectual property protection and counteraction to monopolistic activities. - Minsk : Amalfeya, 2011. - C. 136-155.

52. DOOR. Agriculture and Rural Development *II* [Electronic resource]. - 2017. - Mode of access:
http://ec.europa.eu/agriculture/quality/door/list.html?&recordStart=0&filter .dossier Number=&filter.comboName=&filterMin.milestone_mask=&filterMin.milestone =&filterMax.milestone_mask=&filterMax.milestone=&filter.country=DE&filter. category=&filter.type=PDO&filter.status= . - Date of access: 05.10.2017.

53. DOOR. Agriculture and Rural Development *II* [Electronic resource]. - 2017. - Mode of access:
http://ec.europa.eu/agriculture/quality/door/list.html;jsessionid=pLOhLqqLXhNmF QyFllb24mY3t9dJQPflg3xbL2YphGT4k6zdWn34!- 370879141?&recordStart =0&filter. dossierNumber=&filter.comboName=&filterMi n .milestonemask=&filterMin.milestone=&filterMax.milestone_mask=&filter ax.milestone= &filter.country= DE&filter.category=&filter.type=PGI&filter.status= REGISTERED . - Date of access: 05.10.2017.

54. Civil Code of the Russian Federation (Part Four) of 18.12.2006 N 230-FZ (ed. of 08.12.2011) *And* SPS ConsultantPlus [Electronic resource] / LLC "Yurspectr". - M., 2017.

55. The Treaty on the Eurasian Economic Union (together with Annexes 1-33) (Signed in Astana 29.05.2014) *I* SPS ConsultantPlus [Electronic resource] / LLC "Yurspectr". - M., 2017.

56. Sergeev, A.P. Intellectual Property Law in the Russian Federation / AL. Sergeev, 2nd ed., revision and supplement. - Moscow: TC Velby, 2003. - 752 c.

57. Dozortsev, V.A. Objects of exclusive rights / V.A. Dozortsev // Intellectual Rights. Concept, system, tasks of codification *I* V.A. Dozortsev; Research Centre of Private Law. - M. :Statut, 2003. - 416 c.

58. Conclusion of the Board of the Chamber of Patent Disputes from 11.03.2013 : an appendix to the decision of the Federal Service for Intellectual Property from 08.05.2013 on the application №2012703911 *And* SPS ConsultantPlus [Electronic resource] / LLC "Yurspectr". - M., 2017.

59. Gorlenko, S.A. Kiriy, L.L. Improvement of legislation in the field of appellations of origin of goods and geographical indications / S.A. Gorlenko, L.L. Kiriy // Patents and Licences. - 2013. - № 12. - C. 13-19.

60. Kovalchuk, O.O. The right of telektualno! property on geographical designation

in YKpaiii and the European Union crashes : civic-legal aspect : author's dissertation on obtaining a scientific degree of candidate of jurisprudence : speciality. 12.00.03 "Civil Law and Civil Procedure; Family Law; International Private Law / O.O. Kovalchuk. - Kshv. - 2014. - 19 c.

61. Register No. 39 // Official web-portal of the State Service of Intellectual Property Rights of Ukraine [Electronic resource]. - 2017. - Mode of access: http://sips.gov.ua/i_upload/file/39.pdf- Date of access: 05.10.2017.

62. Verordnung (EG) Nr. 207/2009 des Rates vom 26. Februar 2009 fib die Gemeinschaftsmarke *11* EUR-Lex [Electronic resource]. - 2017. - Access mode: http://eur-lex.europa.eu/legal-content/DE/TXT/?qid=1410977305309&uri=CELEX:02009R0207-20130701 - Date of access: 05.10.2017.

63. Geografische Herkunftsbezeichnungen als Marketingtool *11* SKW Schwarz [Electronic resource]. - 2017. - Mode of access:
https ://www .skwschwarz .de/ aktuelles/artikel/artikel-detail/news/geographical-indications-of-origin-as-a-marketing-tool/_/detail/News/. Date of access: 05.10.2017.

64. Gorlenko, C.A., Korchagin, DA. Trademark: grounds for refusal in registration / S.A. Gorlenko, D.A. Korchagin // Patents and Licences. - 2004. - № 2. - C. 44-50.

65. On approval of recommendations on certain issues of examination of claimed designations: Order of Rospatent, 23 March 2001 № 39 / // CGC ConsultantPlus [Electronic resource] / LLC "Yurspectr". - M., 2017.

66. Civil Law. In 3 vol. T. 3 : textbook / E.Nabramova, N.Naverchenko, YuV Baigusheva; ed. by AL Sergeyev. - Moscow : Prospect, 2010. -880 c.

67. Grishaev, SL. Intellectual property: textbook / SL.Grishaev. - Moscow: Yurist. - 2004. - 240 c.

68. Gavrilov E.L., Danilina E.A. Commentary to the Law of the Russian Federation "On trademarks, service marks and appellations of origin of goods" / EL. Gavrilov, E.A. Danilina. - Izd-vo "Ekzamen", M.: 2004.

69. Frolova, N.M. The name of places of origin of goods as an object of legal protection *And* Collection of scientific papers in memory of V.A. Ryasentsev. - M., 1995. C. 75-89.

70. Civil law : textbook : in 3 vol. VOL.3 / V.V. Bezbakh, D.A.Belova [et al] ; ed. by V.L.Mozolin. - 2nd ed., rev. and supplement. - M. : Prospect, 2014.-704 p.

71. Zykov, S.V. Atypical exclusive rights / S.V. Zykov *I* Tsivilist. 2011. - № 3. C. 66 - 68

72. Schwarz, F. Der Schutz geographischer Herkunftsangaben / F.Schwarz. - GRIN Verlag, 2003.

73. Kolesnikova, V.V.. Means of individualisation of participants of civil turnover and goods (work, services) produced by them as objects of intellectual property rights: autoref. dis. ... k-ta jurid. sciences: 12.00.03 / V.V. Kolesnikova - Astana, 2007. - 30 c.

74. Ley de la Propiedad Industrial (modificada hasta el 9 de abril de 2012) *I* WIPO Intellectual Property Law and Treaties Database (WIPO Lex) // World Intellectual Property

Organisation [Electronic resource].   - 2017. - Mode of access: http://www.wipo.int/wipolex/en/text.jsp?file_id=264465. - Date of access: 05.10.2017.

75.   Kovalchuk, O.O. The right of geographical property on geographical designation in Ukraine and the European Union countries : civil-legal aspect : author's thesis for the degree of Candidate of Jurisprudence : speciality. 12.00.03 "Civil law and civil procedure; family law; international private law / O.O. Kovalchuk. - Kshv. -2014.-19c.

76.   Dmitrichenko, G.M. Legal regime of geographical and other designation in Ukraine as an object of industrial property! : author's thesis for the award of the scientific degree of candidate of jurisprudence : speciality. 12.00.03 "Civic law and civic process; family law; international private law / G.M. Dmitrichenko. - Kshv.-2014.-18 p.

77.   Gorlenko S.A., Eremenko V.I. Commentary to the Law of the Russian Federation "On trademarks, service marks and appellations of origin of goods" *and* Commentary to the legislation on intellectual property protection / Under general ed. by V.I. Eremenko. M., 1997.

78.   Dozortsev, V.A. Subjects of exclusive rights / V.A. Dozortsev *And* Intellectual Rights: Notion. System. Codification tasks : collection of articles / Research Centre of Private Law. - Moscow: "Statut", 2003. - 416 c.

79.   Gorodov, O.A. The right to means of individualisation (trademarks, service marks, appellations of origin of goods, trade names, commercial designations) / O.A. Gorodov. Gorodov. - Moscow: Wolters Kluwer Russia, 2006. - 427 c.

80.   Pro ochorona prava na znazhennya znachennya pokhodzhennya khodokhodnya: Zakona Ukraina, 16 June 1999 *i* Zakodavstvo Ukraina [Electronic resource]. - 2017.   - Mode of access: http://zakon2.rada.gov.ua/laws/show/752-14/print1218034688041545. - Date of access: 05.10.2017.

81.   Law on Appellations of Origin and Geographical Indications of Goods: Law of Georgia, date, number [Electronic resource] *And* Sakpatent - 2017. - Access mode: http http://www.sakpatenti.gov.ge/en/page/61/. - Date of access: 05.10.2017.

82.   Uvarkin, G. System of means of individualisation: stages of formation and modernity / G. Uvarkin // Intellectual Property. Industrial property. - 2008. - № 8. - C. 13-18.

83.   Stem, St. Are GIs IP? *11* E.I.P.R. - 2007. - Vol. 29. - № 2. - P. 39^12

84.   WT/DS174/R European communities - protection of trademarks and geographical indications for agricultural products and foodstuffs / World trade organisation [Electronic resource]. - 2017. - Access mode: https://www.wto.org/english/tratop_e/dispu_e/174r_e.pdf - Date of access: 05.10.2017.

85. 0 trademarks, service marks and appellations of origin of goods: Law of the Republic of Kazakhstan, 26 July 1999, № 456 / National Patent Office Republik of Kazakhstan [Electronic resource]. - 2017. - Access mode : http://adilet.zan.kz/rus/docs/Z990000456_. - Date of access: 05.10.2017.

86. Berkhart, G. Trademarks and appellations of origin of goods in the fourth part of the Civil Code / G. Berkhart // Patents and Licences - 2007. - №3.

Buy your books fast and straightforward online - at one of world's fastest growing online book stores! Environmentally sound due to Print-on-Demand technologies.

Buy your books online at
www.morebooks.shop

Kaufen Sie Ihre Bücher schnell und unkompliziert online – auf einer der am schnellsten wachsenden Buchhandelsplattformen weltweit! Dank Print-On-Demand umwelt- und ressourcenschonend produzi ert.

Bücher schneller online kaufen
www.morebooks.shop